Rain Forests

A Pro/Con Issue

Linda Carlson Johnson

HOT
PRO/CON
ISSUES

Enslow Publishers, Inc.

40 Industrial Road   PO Box 38
Box 398   Aldershot
Berkeley Heights, NJ 07922   Hants GU12 6BP
USA   UK

http://www.enslow.com

Library of Congress Cataloging-in-Publication Data

Johnson, Linda Carlson, 1949–
    Rain forests : a pro/con issue / Linda Carlson Johnson.
        p. cm. — (Hot pro/con issues)
    Includes bibliographical references (p. 60) and index.
    Summary: Describes tropical rain forests and discusses different issues surrounding their destruction, including species extinction, land rights of tribal peoples, economic pressures of developing countries, and global warming.
    ISBN 0-7660-1202-6
    1. Rain forest ecology—Juvenile literature. 2. Rain forests—Juvenile literature. 3. Rain forest conservation—Juvenile literature. 4. Deforestation—Tropics—Juvenile literature. [1. Rain forests. 2. Rain forest ecology. 3. Ecology. 4. Rain forest conservation.] I. Title. II. Series.
QH541.5.R27J64   1999
577.34—dc21   98-34060
                                     CIP
                                     AC

Printed in the United States of America

10 9 8 7 6 5 4 3 2 1

To Our Readers:
All Internet addresses in this book were active and appropriate when we went to press. Any comments or suggestions can be sent by e-mail to Comments@enslow.com or to the address on the back cover.

Illustration Credits: AP\Wide World Photos, pp. 21, 32, 36, 38, 41, 50; © Corel Corporation, pp. 1, 4, 5, 8, 13, 18, 24, 58.

Cover Illustration: © Corel Corporation

Contents

Could people drain all the water out of the oceans? Could they flatten the Rocky Mountains? Could they destroy the world's vast tropical rain forests?

As recently as forty years ago, the answers to each of these questions would have been the same: "That's impossible!" Even today, we would laugh at the idea that oceans could turn into deserts. We would never believe that the Rockies could be knocked down. But the idea that the world's tropical rain forests could be destroyed has become all too possible.

Tropical rain forests are disappearing so fast that some scientists say they could be wiped out within our lifetime. The trees are falling to chain saws, bulldozers, and fires set by people. In 1987 alone, so many fires were burning in the rain forests of South America that much of the continent was covered by a thick cloud of smoke. A man living in southern Brazil said, "the sky appeared gray with smoke, the sun was weak and dark red and disappeared long before it touched the horizon in the evening."[1]

When people in other parts of the world heard this news, they became alarmed. Scientists warned that millions of plants and animals could become extinct if rain forests were lost. As forests disappear, the amount of carbon dioxide gas, which trees "breathe" just as we breathe oxygen, increases. This extra gas threatens to trap too much heat in the atmosphere and change climates all over the world. Once the land is stripped bare, scientists say, more disaster could come. Floods could wash soil into rivers and streams, killing fish. And some land would bake in the hot tropical sun and turn into desert.

The solution to all these problems seems obvious—stop cutting down and burning rain forests. But before we get out our fire hoses, we need to understand the struggle that is going on beneath the smoke of rain forest fires.

People are not destroying rain forests because they want to harm the environment. They are cutting down and burning trees because they are in a desperate struggle to improve their lives. They cut down trees so they can sell them. Or they clear the

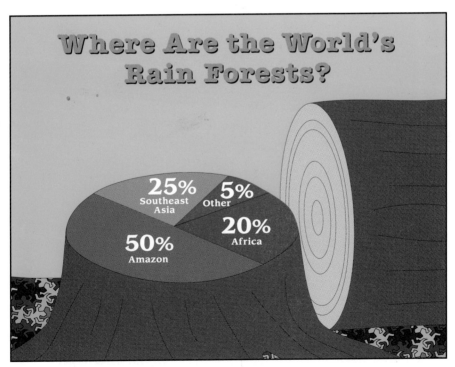

Source: Kenton Miller and Laura Tangley, *Trees of Life: Saving Tropical Forests and Their Biological Wealth* (Boston: Beacon Press, 1991).

land to make way for roads, farms, cattle ranches, and mines. Often, these projects are supported by the governments of rain forest countries and by big banks and businesses in other parts of the world.

Now we must ask another question: "Can a way be found to help people and save rain forests at the same time?" We may say, "That's impossible!" Only by learning much more about why rain forests are being destroyed, about the people who live in rain forest countries, and about the rain forests themselves, can we ever hope to discover how the impossible might yet be possible.

Chapter 1

What Is a Tropical Rain Forest?

Come to a tropical rain forest in South America. On the forest floor, it is almost always warm and damp and dark. The trees stretch skyward like great long telephone poles, reaching as high as twenty-story skyscrapers. A giant, furry, slow-moving animal called a two-toed sloth climbs slowly up a tree trunk. In the crooks of the trees, large plants called *bromeliads* act like buckets to catch rain dripping from the branches above. Snails, worms, crabs, frogs, and beetles make their homes in these hanging water wells, and birds and bats are drawn to their flowers. High overhead, howler monkeys scream and swing quickly through the trees. Brightly colored parrots and toucans hunt for fruit and insects to eat. Spectacular butterflies float through the air.

This type of forest is not like the woods most of us in North America know. The woods we know are the forests of *temperate* regions. These forests are found north and south of imaginary lines around the globe called the Tropic of Cancer and the Tropic of Capricorn. In these temperate regions, it is winter when the earth tilts away from the sun and summer when the earth tilts toward the sun. Temperate forests, which change with the seasons, are found in North America, Europe, parts of South America, eastern Asia, and New Zealand.[1]

Tropical regions are located in a wide belt near the equator, the imaginary line that circles the globe at its widest point. The tropical belt stretches north and south from the equator to the Tropic of Cancer and Tropic of Capricorn. The area inside the belt is called "tropical" or "the tropics" because it is between these two lines. There, the sun's rays are always very intense. The tropics do not have four seasons as other parts of the world do. In temperate regions, for example, days are shorter and colder in the winter and longer and warmer in the summer. But in tropical regions, the sun rises and sets at about the same times year-round, and the temperature is always warm. In parts of the tropics where there are no trees, the intense sun creates scorching heat and desert conditions. But in forested areas, the shaded areas below the trees stay a steady 75 to 85 degrees Fahrenheit just about every day, all year long.

*T*ropical rain forests are home to colorful and exotic creatures, such as the green-cheeked Amazon parrot.

Most tropical rain forests are not only warm but also very rainy or wet. Some tropical rain forests, called *cloud* forests, are high in the mountains, where mists, clouds, and rain keep them moist. *Lowland* tropical rain forests receive their moisture from extremely heavy rainfall—anywhere from 80 to 400 inches of rain per year.[2] In the United States, there are some places, such as New Orleans, Louisiana, where normal annual rainfall reaches sixty inches. But most spots in the United States receive about thirty to forty inches of rain a year. And some receive far less. Phoenix, Arizona, for example, and Las Vegas, Nevada, usually receive less than ten inches of rain each year.[3]

There are some rain forests outside the tropics. One is in the Pacific Northwest of the United States, for example. But because these rain forests are in *temperate* regions, the animals and plants in these forests are very different from those found in tropical rain forests.

Life in the Forests

If you took a short walk through a temperate forest with a guidebook to identify trees, plants, birds, insects, and other animals, you would have no problem listing in a small notebook everything you saw. You might identify three to four species of trees, and if you had an eagle eye, about twenty to thirty types of birds.

You would need many more notebooks than you could carry if you tried the same kind of nature walk in a tropical rain forest. Even if you had a guidebook, it would not help you much. Tropical rain forests cover only about 6 percent of Earth's surface, but they are home to at least 50 percent of all the species of plants and animals on the planet.[4] Many of these millions of species have never been identified. Scientists know this is true because in just about every new area of tropical rain forest they explore, they find species that no one has ever seen before.

There is another big difference in what you would find if your class tried nature walks in temperate and tropical rain forests. If your class decided to split up into small groups, with each group exploring an acre of temperate forest, you would likely come up with the same basic list of plants and animals. If one group identified birch trees, brown squirrels, daddy longlegs spiders, and cardinals, the other groups probably would also find those same plants and animals. But if your class did the same exercise in a tropical rain forest, the groups' lists might be wildly different. Scientists have found as many as seven hundred species of trees in a single acre of rain forest[5] and as many as fifty-four types of ants on just one tree![6] And not every acre of rain forest is alike. Scientists exploring rain forests often come upon new types of beetles, butterflies, or frogs that they have never seen before and that they believe may live only in that one small part of the rain forest.[7]

This level of *biodiversity*—a wide variety of plants and animals in an environment—makes tropical rain forests unique and very delicate. Cutting down even a few acres of tropical rain forest can mean wiping out species of animals and plants that live nowhere else on Earth.[8]

A Delicate Food Web

Every type of *biome*, or special environment on earth—from desert to deep ocean to tropical rain forest—has a *food web*. In a food web, sometimes

A Killer Tree Full of Life

In the rain forests of Central America lives a tree with two scary names. The people of Costa Rica and Panama call it "matapalo," which means tree-killer. Scientists know it by its more common, but no less violent name, the strangler fig.

This tall rain forest tree is not actually a tree at all, although it grows taller than most trees and spreads out like a huge umbrella when it reaches the forest canopy. There, it bears fruit, sweet sticky figs that are a favorite food for fruit bats, parrots, macaws, and spider monkeys.

As these animals swoop, swing, and soar through the trees, they drop their waste throughout the forest canopy. In that waste are the sticky seeds of the strangler fig. The seeds do not need to fall to the ground to sprout. A seed that lands in the crook of a tree branch uses decaying plants, fungi, and lichens growing there as its "soil." Once the seed bursts open, it grows rapidly, sending long, stringlike vines toward the earth. Along the way, these vines attach themselves to the tree's trunk. When the vines reach the ground, they form a network of shallow roots, then sprout new vines that will make the long journey back up to the canopy and sunlight.

The matapalo's vines wind up around the tree, twine through the canopy, and send even more vines downward to earth. Gradually, the matapalo "strangles" the tree that has been supporting it. The matapalo's roots, high in the trees and on the ground, take nutrition away from the tree. And the pressure of the thickening vines prevents the tree trunk from growing any wider. The tree rots and dies, leaving the matapalo standing alone, with a hollow "trunk" of thick vines and "branches" of fig-laden vines providing abundant food for hungry monkeys and birds.

Source: Adrian Forsyth and Kenneth Miyata, *Tropical Nature* (New York: Charles Scribner's Sons, 1984), pp. 54-56.

called a *food chain*, plants and animals depend on one another to survive. In a temperate forest, squirrels, mice, rabbits, and small birds feed on nuts, seeds, plants, and insects. The smaller animals, in turn, provide food for larger ones. For example, hawks and owls hunt small birds and mice, and foxes feed on animals such as mice and rabbits.

In a temperate forest, if a fairly small area of trees is cut down or destroyed by fire, the different species of that forest usually survive. Even if many individual animals and plants are killed, the same species of animals and plants still live in most other parts of the forest. But in a tropical rain forest, many species live in only one small area. In the rain forests of South America, scientists found one type of wasp, for example, that pollinates just one type of fig tree.[9] If all the fig trees of that species are destroyed in a fire, then that type of wasp cannot survive. Both species become *extinct*, which means they no longer live anywhere on Earth. In recent years, as large sections of tropical rain forests throughout the world have been destroyed, countless species of animals and plants have become extinct.

What Is Under the Forests?

Another difference between tropical rain forests and temperate forests is their soil types. The soil under most temperate forests is rich and deep. The roots of most temperate forest trees are thick and stretch far into the soil, where they draw nourishment from water and minerals. After a forest fire in a temperate forest, new tree seedlings can quickly take root in the rich soil.

The problem of cutting down or burning even fairly small areas of forested land is an especially serious one for tropical rain forests. In many tropical regions, once a forest is cut down, nothing will grow there. That is because the soil in most tropical rain forests is so thin and poor.

For a long time, even scientists did not understand this fact. They assumed, because tropical rain forests were so dense and full of life, that they could regrow easily if they were cut down. But in recent years, scientists have come to understand that in most tropical rain forests, the trees have very shallow roots. They depend not on the soil but on a rich mat of tiny organisms called *fungi*. These fungi break down the litter on the forest floor—leaves, dead insects, and animal wastes. The fungi then deliver the chemicals from this digested litter to the roots of the trees.[10] When a tropical rain forest is destroyed by fire, the fungi mat that provided food for the trees is gone, and the poor soil cannot provide enough nutrients for trees.

*T*hough the woolly monkey is one of the more well-known rain forest animals, there are other species that have not even been discovered yet.

Life in Layers

Botanists identify several layers of life in both temperate and tropical rain forests. In a temperate forest, the richest layer is often on the *forest floor*, where moles and other small animals build tunnels in the rich soil and insects, worms, and bacteria feed on fallen leaves. A temperate forest also has an *herb layer* of plants, such as ferns and moss, which carpets the forest floor. Next come the *shrub layer* of bushes and other plants, the *understory* of smaller trees, and finally, a *canopy* of taller trees.[11]

A tropical rain forest has layers, too. At ground level, on the forest floor, live many crawling creatures—centipedes, scorpions, and hairy tarantulas. You might also find a few snakes, birds, and insect-eating rodents like the fat capybara (in South America).[12]

Go up one "flight" to the understory, where some shrubs and small trees manage to grow in the shady forest, and you will find many kinds of insects, along with snakes and tree-climbing cats, such as jaguars and leopards. In the rain forests of Australia and Papua New Guinea, you might even see a tree kangaroo![13]

The next stop is the canopy. Here, the trees spread their leaves to gather as much of the tropical sun and rain as they can. Their tops, or *crowns*, often come together, forming a thick, green umbrella that cuts off the sun from the forest layers below. The canopy also catches much of the heavy rain that falls year-round. Far below the canopy, people and animals can roam the forest floor without getting drenched, even though it is raining high above them.

In the canopy, you will find the plants and animals that most people think of when they imagine a rain forest. Here, monkeys chatter and parrots squawk as they search for fruit and nuts to eat. Thousands of varieties of insects, from the tiniest of ants to seven-inch-long Hercules beetles, patrol tree branches. Colorful butterflies flit in and out of shade

Layers of the Rain Forest

Emergent layer

Canopy

Understory

Forest floor

and sunlight. Giant vines wind through the trees, growing toward the light. And many plants called *epiphytes* grow in the crooks and along the trunks of trees. Some of these plants, such as mistletoe, are *parasites* that draw the life from trees. Others, such as bromeliads, form large "baskets" of leaves that catch the falling rain and provide homes for insects. Still other epiphytes have long, dangling roots that gather minerals directly from the mist and from decaying leaves among the tree branches. Brilliant flowers such as orchids drape tree branches like ornaments.[14]

Vines and trees that push above the sun-and-shade-dappled canopy face very harsh conditions. Here, in the *emergent* layer, the sun's rays are intense, the rains pour down in torrents, and the winds often blow in gales. Plants and animals that venture into this uppermost layer have to be tough to survive.[15] When a tree's branches shoot above the canopy into the emergent layer, they often grow much smaller leaves that won't be as easily torn apart by the wind and blowing rain. In the canopy below, the same tree might have much larger leaves that can catch as much sunlight and rain as possible.

The tropical rain forest, with its rich layers of life, is not much like the woods we are familiar with in North America. Scientists want the chance to uncover the secrets that tropical rain forests hold. But they are racing against time.

Chapter 2

Who Owns the Forests?

When we think of a tropical rain forest, most of us imagine a wild, remote jungle that people would dare to enter only at their own risk. We think of it as the place where Tarzan swings through the trees, where rivers are teeming with flesh-eating piranhas, and where jaguars and boa constrictors lie in wait for unsuspecting victims.

That tropical rain forest is a myth. For perhaps thousands of years, people have made their homes in rain forests. These tribal, or *indigenous*, peoples often live deep in the forest, where there are no supermarkets, housing developments, department stores, hospitals, or schools. Some tribes are hunter-gatherers, who hunt animals and gather fruits and nuts from the forest to eat. The largest remaining group of rain forest hunter-gatherers is the Pygmies of Africa, who number 150,000 to 200,000. Other rain forest tribes are farmers. They use a method called *shifting cultivation*, which means that they move from one small field to the next in the forest to plant crops.[1] Whether they are hunter-gatherers or farmers, each tribal group knows how to use the forest to provide for all their needs. They use wood and vines to build homes, wild cotton plants and dyes made from plants for clothing, and all sorts of leaves, roots, and herbs for medicines.

You might say that the tribal peoples of the rain forest have first rights to the land there. Most of these people are not citizens of any country, and the territory where they hunt and farm often stretches across the borders of nations. But every acre of rain forest in the world also belongs to a particular country, where many people live who are not tribal forest dwellers.

Most of those countries are part of the *developing* world. Countries such as the United States, Japan, and the nations of Europe are part of the *developed* world, where most people live in homes that have running water, electricity, and telephones. In the developed world, many people drive cars on roads that will take them just about anywhere they want to go. Many people work in factories and offices and earn money to buy food, clothing, and things like televisions and computers.

In the developing world, life is much more of a struggle for most people. In the countries of the developing world, a large number of people live in poverty. Many do not have simple things that we take for granted, such as running water, electricity, cars, or even roads. Most people either have very low-paying jobs or are trying to survive by living off the land.

Demands on Rain Forest Land

When most citizens of developing countries think about the rain forest growing on their land, they do not imagine a romantic place to find adventure. Instead, they see a very real forest that is either standing in the way of progress or waiting to be used to help them.

➤ As populations and poverty have grown in rain forest countries, governments have encouraged people to move out of the cities and cut down the rain forests so that the land can be used for farms, cattle ranches, and mines. What has often happened in those nations is that a small number of wealthy landowners end up controlling most of the rain forest land that is cleared. In one state of Brazil called Rondonia, 61 percent of the land is owned by just 2 percent of the people.[2]

➤ In Indonesia, a nation made up of many islands, the main islands where people live became so overcrowded that government officials decided on a drastic measure. Between 1950 and 1989, they moved more than 2 million people from the densely popu-lated islands of Java, Lombok, and Bali to more remote islands, such as Borneo, Sumatra, and New Guinea. People quickly cut down rain forests so they could farm the land. In the four years from 1986 to 1990, about 7 million acres of rain forest land was cleared on Borneo land alone.[3] That is an area about the size of the state of Maryland.

➤ In the rain forest countries of Southeast Asia, the trees themselves were—and still are—in high demand in world markets, especially in Japan and the United States.[4] In Japan, about 60 percent of imported rain forest wood, even high-quality woods like teak and mahogany, is used for cheap plywood. Tropical hardwoods are also used to make fine furniture, paneling, wood salad bowls, and many other products.[5] So logging became big business, and the forests began disappearing at an alarming rate.

Each of these development plans is based on the idea that the land within a nation's borders can be used as that nation sees fit—to provide income, homes, or food for its people.

Help From Big Banks

Beginning in the 1970s, many rain forest countries around the world received outside help for their development plans from international banks. To these banks, lending money to rain forest countries was a good investment. If rain forest lands could be developed, the banks reasoned, these countries would have a chance to lift their people out of poverty. If people could make more money, the countries could not only pay back their bank debt but also might become important new trading partners for the rest of the world.[6]

Concerns of Scientists

As banks lent more and more money to rain forest countries, these banks could claim, along with tribal people and the governments of rain forest countries, that they "owned" the rain forests.

Soon, the rain forests began to disappear at such a rapid rate that scientists and environmentalists

*H*ere, a logging truck hauls lumber in Malaysia. Asian logging companies are rapidly stripping millions of acres of the world's richest ecosystem.

began to raise an alarm. They said, in effect, the rain forests belong to the world, and no one has a right to destroy them.

For one thing, they pointed out, rain forest plants and animals had already provided many important medicines that had improved people's lives—and in some cases, even saved lives. Biologists were working as fast as they could to find out how other rain forest plants and animals might be used. But with an estimated ten thousand species facing extinction each year worldwide by the early 1990s because of rain forest destruction, the scientists feared they were fighting a losing battle.[7]

Some scientists were concerned for another reason. Rain forests, they said, are important to the overall health of the planet. As forests are destroyed, the lands beneath them are exposed to the hot tropical sun and drenching rains.[8] With no trees to hold the thin layer of soil in place, it washes away into rivers, streams, and oceans. The mud in the rivers chokes plants and fish. In the oceans, delicate coral reefs are destroyed. These coral reefs are the breeding grounds for thousands of species of fish.

Global Warming

Other scientists worried that rain forest destruction might be contributing to *global warming*, or climate change, a problem that could affect everyone on Earth. From 1860 to 1960, the average temperature on the planet increased by about 1 degree Celsius.[9] That might not seem like much of an increase, but consider that during the last Ice Age, when glaciers covered much of the Earth, the temperature was only about 3 to 9 degrees cooler than it was in 1860![10]

Disappearing Forests

By 1990, more than half of the world's rain forests had been cut down or burned.[1] Scientists estimate that one to 2 percent or more of the world's remaining rain forests are lost each year. If the destruction continues at that rate, all of the forests could be gone within the next century, perhaps as early as 2050.[2]

In some countries, the rain forests are already gone or nearly wiped out. Ethiopia in Africa, Bangladesh and Thailand in Asia, and the Philippines in the Pacific Ocean are four countries that were once covered by rain forests.[3]

In other countries, rain forests are disappearing rapidly. The Ivory Coast in Africa has the world's highest rate of rain forest destruction, with 5 percent of the forest being lost each year. At that rate, all of the rain forests in that country will be gone by the year 2018.[4]

As rain forests are cut down, an estimated ten thousand species of animals and plants become extinct each year.[5] Some scientists estimate that one rain forest species becomes extinct every fifteen minutes.[6]

[1]John Terbough, *Diversity and the Tropical Rain Forest* (New York: Scientific American Library, 1992) p. 187; [2]Judith Gradwohl and Russell Greenberg, *Saving the Tropical Forests* (London: Earthscan Publications Limited, 1988), p. 33; [3]*Zoo Guides: The Rain Forest* (CD) (San Diego, Calif.: REMedia, Inc., 1994); [4]Kenton Miller and Laura Tangley, *Trees of Life: Saving Tropical Forests and Their Biological Wealth* (Boston: Beacon Press, 1991), p. 93; [5]Bob Reiss, *The Road to Extrema* (New York: Summit Books, 1992), p. 30; [6]Alex Shoumatoff, *The World Is Burning* (Boston: Little, Brown, 1990), p. 341.

Earth is like a large greenhouse, with a layer of gases in the atmosphere acting like a greenhouse roof to trap heat. In a greenhouse, the sun's rays pass through the glass roof, but the glass traps the heat of the sun to help the plants grow. The gases in Earth's atmosphere act in much the same way as the greenhouse glass does. The sun's rays pass through this layer and strike Earth's surface. Some of the heat from the rays is absorbed by the earth. The rest of the heat is reflected back into the atmosphere. To test this idea, think about what it is like to walk barefoot in the summer. If you are walking on black pavement, which absorbs the sun's heat, your feet will quickly feel very hot. But if you step on a

*G*rowing amounts of carbon dioxide are causing Earth's temperature to become too warm. Carbon dioxide is released by the burning of fossil fuels, such as the gasoline used by automobiles.

white sidewalk, which reflects light, you will be able to walk comfortably because much of the heat is rising back into the air. The heat that rises from Earth's surface is trapped in the atmosphere by *greenhouse gases*, such as carbon dioxide. If greenhouse gases did not exist, Earth would be a very cold place.

Some scientists worry that today, Earth is in danger of becoming too warm because the amount of carbon dioxide in the atmosphere is growing. The main reason for this increase in carbon dioxide is the burning of coal and fossil fuels, such as the gasoline used in cars. But another reason for the increase—which threatens to heat up Earth's "greenhouse" too much—is the destruction of rain forests, especially in the Amazon. The burning of forests sends some carbon dioxide into the atmosphere. And living trees absorb large amounts of carbon dioxide. If the trees are gone, some scientists say, the extra carbon dioxide will build up in the atmosphere and trap too much heat.

Scientists do not all agree about just how hot the planet could get as a result of global warming, but they say that if the Earth warms up by as little as 3 degrees Celsius, it could cause major problems. The polar ice caps could melt, for example, and many coastal areas could flood. Increased temperatures could cause drastic changes in climate. Areas that are now farmland could become desert, which would mean a big reduction in the world's food supplies.[11]

For all these reasons, scientists say, all the countries of the world must have a say in what happens to rain forests.

Who owns the rain forests? Is it the tribal peoples, who have lived there for thousands of years and want to continue to hunt animals and gather and raise food on rain forest land? Is it the governments of rain forest countries, who want to clear rain forests so they can build roads, cities, and factories that will provide jobs and a better life for their people? Is it the international banks, who have lent so much money to poor rain forest countries in hopes that they would one day pay the money back as they find ways to use rain forest land in profitable ways? Or is it the scientists and environmentalists, who want to stop rain forest destruction because they believe it could affect the whole planet?

These questions are almost impossible to answer because every group has an important claim. As people worldwide struggle with the issue of rain forest destruction, it is important to consider each claim.

Chapter 3

"A Land Without People for a People Without Land"

There is a tropical rain forest so vast that it is hard to understand how it ever could be destroyed. Half of the world's remaining rain forests are part of this one enormous system sprawling along the Amazon River and its thousands of tributaries.[1] Sometimes called Amazonia, this rain forest stretches across many countries in South America. If Amazonia were a country, it would be the ninth largest on Earth.[2]

Until about forty years ago, most of Amazonia remained untouched. But from 1960 to 1989, more than one tenth of the rain forests in the region were destroyed.[3] Many of those forests were in Brazil, a nation that has more acres of rain forest than any other on Earth.

Settlers From Europe

Brazil and the countries of the Amazon forest surrounding it were once populated only by tribal peoples, who have lived in the forests for at least twenty thousand years. At one time, scientists estimate, as many as 2.5 million tribal people lived in the Amazon rain forest. But their numbers began to drop very quickly after Europeans arrived in South America in the 1500s. The Europeans brought diseases, such as smallpox, that wiped out a large part of the Indian population. Today in the Amazon, only about one hundred thousand tribal people still survive.

A Portuguese navigator was the first European to reach Brazil. Over the following centuries, settlers from Portugal poured into the area. They brought with them large numbers of African slaves. The descendants of these people form the largest part of Brazil's current population of about 150 million.[4]

Plans to Spread West

After World War II ended in 1945, Brazil had a military government. The generals who ran the country wanted to hold onto power. Most of the nation's people lived in poverty in overcrowded cities along the Atlantic coast. The generals reasoned that if they could move settlers into the "wild west" of the Amazon, they could improve the economy—and strengthen their own control over the land.[5]

The government offered money to investors, such as cattle ranchers, who would move into the Amazon to clear and develop the land. To help the ranchers do that, the government began building roads into the wilderness. These road projects drew many poor people who were in search of jobs and land. Because they resented the government giving away land to people who already had money, the poor people formed small armies and began to fight against the government and the wealthy landowners. The government's first attempt to control the Amazon ended in bloody battles.[6]

But the government was not willing to give up on development. In 1970, the generals hatched a new plan, to build roads into the rain forest and give away 250-acre plots of land to people who would be willing to farm.[7] The government launched an advertising campaign on television and in newspapers to encourage people to move into the rain forest. The advertisements called the Amazon "A Land Without People for a People Without Land."[8]

People did move into the forest in hopes of starting new lives. But very few were successful, for a number of reasons:

> ➤ The settlers were not prepared for the harsh conditions they found deep in the forest. Once they cleared their land and planted crops, insect pests attacked the crops and the settlers.[9]

Destroying Elephants Destroys Trees

In Ivory Coast, rain forests are in danger not only because trees are being cut down but because many elephants are being killed by big game hunters who hunt them illegally. If all the elephants are wiped out in Ivory Coast, scientists say, it could mean the extinction of thirty kinds of trees—and two species of giant squirrels that make their homes in the trees. Why? Elephants roaming the forest eat the fruit of these trees. When the elephants deposit their waste, sometimes miles away, they also deposit seeds from the fruit they have eaten. Without the elephants, the trees have no way of distributing their seeds in the forest.

Source: Kenton Miller and Laura Tangley, *Trees of Life: Saving Tropical Forests and Their Biological Wealth* (Boston: Beacon Press, 1991), p. 95.

➢ The "highways" were really dirt roads. The settlers often could not get their crops to market because the roads were washed out or so muddy that no one could travel on them.[10]

➢ Everyone, including settlers, government officials, and scientists, assumed that the soil in the rain forest would be rich and deep. No one understood at that time that the lush rain forests were supported, not by the soil, but by the vegetation on the forest floor. When settlers cleared the land, they used a method called slash-and-burn. The tribal peoples of the forest have used this way of farming for thousands of years. They cut down a small area of forest, allow the trees to dry out, and then burn them. They plant crops for several seasons on the land, then leave it behind and allow the forest to fill in the small gap. But when the settlers used slash-and-burn, they cut and burned much larger areas of forest. The ash-covered soil was too poor to support crops for long. When the settlers moved on to cut down more acres of forest, the land they left behind could not regrow as a forest. Instead, it stayed bare or became choked with weeds.[11]

➢ The settlers often could not make enough money from their crops to support their families. They needed extra jobs, but there were none nearby.[12] And the government never followed through on promises to set up services along the highway like hospitals and schools.

➢ The land the government gave away to settlers was not always "a land without people." New highways often cut through tribal lands, so the settlers faced a fight from tribal people.[13]

➤ Cattle ranchers, who seemed to need a never-ending supply of land, often either stole or laid claim to settlers' land.[14]

Cattle Ranching

The biggest cause of rain forest destruction in the Brazilian Amazon—and in many other rain forest countries of South and Central America—has been cattle ranching. Ranchers often cut down many more acres of trees than the farming settlers did. But like the farming settlers, the ranchers found that rain forest soil would not support their cattle for long. Within about ten years, even grass would not grow on the land.[15] If the ranchers wanted to stay in business, they had to clear more land. That was something they had great reason to do. They did not make much money selling their beef, but they did continue to make money from the government for clearing the land. So, many more acres of rain forest went up in smoke.

Gold Fever

The news that the Brazilian Amazon might be rich in something besides wildlife—gold—touched off a gold rush in 1980 much like the one that began in California in 1848. Prospectors set out to find gold in the riverbeds and along the muddy banks of the Amazon River and its tributaries. Small cities sprang up near these rivers, which meant that some rain forest land was lost. But the miners, called *garimpeiros*, caused a far bigger problem for life in the forest. They dredged up soil and ran it through special machines that used mercury, a

*T*he effects of gold mining on Venezuela's portion of the Amazon rain forest have been devastating.

heavy metal, to separate gold from gravel and dirt. The process released mercury into the air and water. The mercury, which is highly poisonous, contaminated the rivers and the fish in them. People who ate the fish and breathed mercury vapor in the air became very ill.[16]

Mining operations for other metals like iron were also a disaster for the environment and people. To dig the huge pit mines, which were usually run by big companies, rain forest land had to be cleared. The furnaces, called *smelters*, that melt the ore needed charcoal to operate. That charcoal was made from rain forest trees, so even more land had to be cleared to feed the furnaces. The burning charcoal itself created air pollution.[17]

Dams

Another development plan the Brazilian government tried was to build hydroelectric power plants by harnessing the rivers of the Amazon. The idea was that electricity would draw factories, and factories would draw people, who would build cities deep in the Amazon forest. Beginning in 1980, with loans from many foreign companies and international banks, engineering companies set out to build the dams.

But most of the dams created environmental and human disaster. When engineers built them, they did not cut down the forests behind them. Instead, they allowed the huge lakes behind the dams to flood the forest. The water drowned the trees and vegetation, which soon began to rot. At one dam on the Suriname River in Brazil, the stench from the rotting vegetation was so bad that workers at the dam had to wear gas masks. Dams in the Amazon have swamped towns and forced tribal peoples as well as wildlife off the land. Great swarms of mosquitoes often made life miserable for people living near the dams. The mosquitoes normally lived high in the trees, where they laid their eggs in the wells of bromeliad plants and gained nourishment from the blood of animals and birds living in the forest canopy. But when the dams swamped the forest with water, the mosquitoes laid their eggs in the still water held behind the dams. Their nearest source of food was now the people who lived around the dams.[18]

By the 1970s and 1980s, all of these "development" plans were destroying rain forests at an incredibly fast rate. And the news of that destruction was about to break on the world scene.

Chapter 4

Battles Over Rain Forests

On some days, fires rage in thousands of places across the vast Amazon basin, following a broad belt where settlers and farmers are beating back the jungle frontier. . . . From the flames, tons of fumes and particles are hurled into the sky, and at night, roaring and red, the forest looks to be at war.

—*The New York Times*, August 12, 1988[1]

The effects are much worse than those from [widespread] bombing. You end up with massive smoke clouds spread over millions of square kilometers. In some places, visibility is so bad you have to wait days for things to clear up if you want to travel by plane or car. There are literally thousands of fires, and I'm just talking about the larger ones.

—*Science* magazine, October 13, 1989, quoting Brazilian space scientist Alberto Setzer[2]

The devastation is just unbelievable. It's one of the greatest tragedies of all history.

—*Time* magazine, September 18, 1989, quoting then–United States senator Al Gore[3]

Before 1987, few people in the United States knew how much of the South American rain forests were being destroyed. In that year, a United States satellite sent back pictures that showed the locations of thousands of fires burning across the Amazon. On the worst day of 1987, September 9, the satellite detected 7,603 separate fires.[4] The smoke from these fires was so thick in places that airplanes could not land without the help of radar.[5]

Once this news became public, the government of the largest Amazon nation, Brazil, came under attack from environmentalists around the world. The scientists charged that Brazil was destroying its own forests and wildlife, harming tribal peoples, and endangering the rest of the world by spewing carbon dioxide into the atmosphere and increasing the danger of global warming. An article titled "Playing with Fire" that appeared in *Time* magazine said, "The whole world has awakened at last to how much is at stake in the Amazon." Once, only a handful of scientists had been sounding the alarm about rain forests. Now, everyone from politicians to television news commentators to rock stars was demanding an end to rain forest destruction.[6]

The outcry put increasing pressure on rain forest nations to do something to stop the destruction. José Sarney, Brazil's president, lashed out in anger. He said the battle over rain forests was really a battle between rich, developed nations and poor, undeveloped nations. The rich nations, he said, with all their cars and factories, created most of the pollution in the world. Besides, he said, the rain forest nations had a right to do whatever they wanted to do with their land.[7]

Tribal Peoples Fight Back

Some of the battles over rain forests were being waged, not between nations, but between groups of

*T*his fire in Brazil happened during a drought in 1998 and was not intentionally started. However, much of the country's rain forest has been burned by ranchers and farmers.

people in the rain forest nations who fought over control of the land. Those battles were often unfair fights because one side had more money or power than the other. Perhaps the most lopsided of these battles has been between tribal peoples who lived in the forests and people who have wanted to cut down the rain forests—often for very good reasons, such as selling trees for income or clearing land for ranches, mines, or farms.

Borneo protests. In 1987, world attention was drawn to the rain forests of the island of Borneo, in Malaysia. (Part of Borneo is in Malaysia and part is in Indonesia.) The year before, Japanese businesses interested in logging forests had worked with the government to build a road through the forest to help doctors reach people who lived deep in the jungle. Once the road was built, it was also used by the logging trucks of the Japanese companies. The road—and the logging—moved into the forest where the Penan tribe lived. Soon the Penan people realized that their way of life was in danger. As trees fell to chain saws and bulldozers, the tribe lost the animals and plants they used for food and their rivers became muddy as rains washed soil into them. Beginning in 1987, the Penan set up block-ades to stop the bulldozers of the logging company.[8]

The government reacted violently. A statement from the Penan people described what happened after a massive blockade in 1993:

> All our huts were torn down with chain saws and burned. When we were disabled by the tear gas, the police and soldiers went on to destroy our barricade, which we had been guarding for nine months. The police had shields and helmets, and they were hitting us without any pity.[9]

The Yanomami versus gold miners. In Brazil, one of the largest groups of native people is the Yanomami. Beginning in 1988, massive numbers of gold miners began invading Yanomami lands. The operation of the mines polluted the rivers, and hungry miners raided the Yanomami's small farms. Violent clashes broke out between the Yanomami and the miners. People on both sides died in the fighting. Some tribespeople who tried to protect their land were murdered. But for the Yanomami, a greater death toll came from diseases, from measles to simple cold viruses, brought in by the miners. The tribespeople also suffered from malnutrition; with so much forest cut down, they lost much of their food supply.[10]

The tragedy of the Yanomami has been repeated all across Amazonia. In some cases, whole tribes have been completely wiped out. A group called

*T*he Pemon Indians of Venezuela use logs to block a highway so that developers and gold miners cannot invade their homeland.

Cultural Survival estimates that in Brazil alone, one tribal society has died out every year since 1900.[11]

Rubber tappers versus large landowners. Tribal peoples were not the only ones living in the rain forests of the Amazon before the government began its great push to settle and develop the land. A large number of people who made their living by tapping rubber trees for *latex* (the material from which rubber is made) had been working in the forest for decades.

In 1839, Charles Goodyear invented *vulcanization*, a process that made latex tough enough to be used in many products. In the last part of the nineteenth century, demand for rubber grew and touched off a "boom" period for Amazonia, the main source for rubber.

Rich landowners bought up rain forest land and hired hundreds of thousands of people to gather latex using a process that does not destroy trees. The rubber tappers, who were poor, were forced to buy all their tools from the landowners, who charged them high prices. The landowners, not the tappers, took the rubber to market and made big profits on it. The rubber tappers became slaves to the landowners.

The great rubber boom ended around 1910, when people in Southeast Asia discovered that they could grow rubber trees on big plantations. Because the latex was so much easier to gather on the plantations, it could be sold more cheaply than Amazon rubber. Many of the Amazonian landowners abandoned their businesses, leaving the rubber tappers on their own.

The rubber tappers in Brazil and other rain forest nations of the Amazon basin continued to work their plots of land, called *seringals*. They managed barely to make a living at it. But in the 1970s and 1980s, they faced a big threat from cattle ranchers, who claimed the tappers' land and wanted to clear it. The rubber tappers organized protests to stop the destruction. They held hands in a long line when the men came with bulldozers and chain saws to clear the forests.

Sometimes these protests worked, but the battle

The Life of a Rubber Tapper

People who tap rubber trees for latex work very hard. When the weather is dry enough, a rubber tapper travels a long, winding trail through the rain forest each day to reach all the rubber trees in his *seringal*, which is his particular area of the forest. For about four hours in the morning, the rubber tapper makes diagonal slices on one hundred or more rubber trees scattered throughout the forest. After he has made a slice or two in the trunk of a tree, he hangs a cup on it to catch the latex that slowly oozes out of the cuts. In the afternoon, the rubber tapper walks the same long trail again, collecting about twelve pounds of latex. Then he goes back home and "cooks" the latex over a smoky fire fueled by palm nuts he has gathered in the forest. He pours the rubber over a kind of wooden paddle until it forms a large ball. When he has a large enough amount of rubber, he takes it to market to sell. Many rubber tappers also gather nuts and fruits from the forest that can help them to add to their income.

Source: Alex Shoumatoff, *The World Is Burning* (Boston: Little, Brown, 1990), pp. 10–11.

between the tappers and ranchers was often deadly. Although government agents were supposed to keep order, many took bribes from the ranchers and looked the other way when troublesome rubber tappers were murdered.

When one of the main organizers of the rubber tappers, Francisco "Chico" Mendes, was shot down in 1988, world attention focused on their plight. The situation has gotten better, but the rubber tappers still struggle to preserve their way of life—and the forest that provides it.

*F*rancisco "Chico" Mendes was an ecologist who fought to save the Amazon jungle. He was shot dead by unidentified gunmen at his home in 1988.

A Losing Battle

In the battle over rain forests, few people have been winners. In countries where rain forests are already gone or rapidly disappearing, people have suffered greatly. In Ethiopia, for example, the land that was once covered by rain forests turned to desert in the hot tropical sun. The people in Ethiopia try to farm the land, but there are frequent droughts. At those times, famine kills thousands of people, especially children. In other nations, such as Thailand, Bangladesh, and the Philippines, heavy rainfall has brought disaster. With no forests to absorb the rain and hold the soil in place, the rains have caused floods and mud slides that have killed many people.

In the Amazon basin and Central America, the

dream of developing rain forest lands became a nightmare. Settlers, unable to grow successful crops on poor rain forest soil, often gave up. Cattle ranching brought money to a few wealthy landowners but created few jobs. The money that the ranchers made did not come mostly from selling beef but from the government, which paid them to keep cutting down more forest. Dams that were supposed to create electricity and booming industries around them simply failed. And mining was polluting rivers.

Governments of rain forest countries were in trouble, too. In Indonesia, foreign companies were gaining profits from the tropical hardwood they sold for such things as furniture and piano keys, but local communities got little of the money.[12] In Latin America, many rain forest countries owed huge amounts of money to international banks. The debt skyrocketed as each new development plan failed.

What Could Be Done?

After rain forest destruction became widely known in the late 1980s, the banks faced increasing pressure from environmentalists, scientists, and many others to stop lending money to nations that cut down or burned their forests. Bank officials did not entirely stop lending money to these countries, but they slowly began to change their policies. They did that not only because of the worldwide pressure but for a practical reason: Rain forest countries were not paying back their loans. The banks began to look for ways that rain forest countries could provide for their people without massive destruction of rain forests.[13]

As for the governments of rain forest countries, most were not completely ready to give up the idea of cutting down rain forests to make way for development, such as timber production, cattle ranching, oil wells, mines, farms, and roads. But they were beginning to realize that most of their large development plans had failed. And they were deep in debt, so they were willing to try something new. But what could that be? The people of rain forest countries would find many answers—and most of them would come from the forests themselves.

Chapter 5

What Is It Worth to Save Rain Forests?

By the 1980s, big banks around the world had lent rain forest countries huge amounts of money to develop their land—to build roads and factories and to clear land for ranches, farms, and mines. But many of the projects had not worked out, and rain forest countries, including Brazil, Indonesia, Madagascar, and Costa Rica, owed hundreds of billions of dollars that they could not pay back. Brazil alone owed $150 billion.[1] Most people in rain forest countries believed that the only chance they had to pay back these huge amounts of money was to clear more rain forest land so they could sell timber, raise crops or cattle that could bring in cash, drill for oil, or mine for gold. Yet many environmentalists, politicians, and even ordinary citizens—both outside and inside rain forest countries—were beginning to realize how important rain forests were to the whole world, and they wanted rain forest destruction to stop. How could that happen, when so many people were depending on that destruction for their survival?

One answer to that question seemed to come

from a scientist named Thomas Lovejoy, who worked with the World Wildlife Fund. In 1984, he sat in the United States Congress, listening to an angry environmentalist from Brazil saying that forests were being destroyed because Brazil owed so much money to international banks. To pay back debt, the environmentalist said, poor countries needed dollars. And to earn dollars, they had to sell forest products like wood and crops raised on cleared rain forest land. As Lovejoy listened to the Brazilian environmentalist, he remembered his recent visit to a rain forest park in Brazil. People were logging in the park because the government did not have enough money to pay park guards. Lovejoy wondered whether there might be a way to reduce the debt of rain forest nations in exchange for protection of the forests.[2]

So began a popular idea called "debt-for-nature swaps." In these deals, environmental groups raise money and "buy" part of a nation's debt. In exchange, the nation agrees to use some money to preserve part of the rain forest. These swaps have helped preserve rain forests in many nations, including Ecuador, Bolivia, Argentina, and Costa Rica. Recently, the United States government has begun to spend some money that would normally be used for foreign aid on debt-for-nature swaps.[3]

Many foreign investors and international banks, like the World Bank, are now being much more careful about setting certain conditions when they lend money to rain forest nations. In 1990, when the World Bank lent money to Brazil for development, for example, it required that millions of acres of forest be set aside for use by tribal peoples and for parks and scientific experiments.[4]

Lessons From Forest People

The Kayapó people of the Amazon use slash-and-burn farming, but they know how to make rain forest soil produce crops for a long time. They begin by cutting down a small area of forest in April or May. Even before the logs dry out and fires are set in August or September, Kayapó women plant sweet potatoes, manioc, and yams that will sprout when the fires die down. Next, the women plant crops that can be harvested in a short time, such as corn, beans, melons and squash, as well as crops such as peppers that can be harvested much later. The women prepare food in the fields, too. They move their cooking fires often and plant new crops in the ashes at each site. They also plant many kinds of fruit trees, which attract animals and birds that are an important part of the Kayapó diet. In their droppings, the animals and birds that wander into the garden also "plant" new seeds.

By careful planting, weeding, and burning, the Kayapó people can use a plot of land for up to twenty-five years. Once they do leave a piece of land behind, the forest begins to grow back. If scientists and farmers could ever fully understand the secrets of the Kayapó, they might gain a better understanding of the rain forests themselves.

Source: Susanna Hecht and Alexander Cockburn, *The Fate of the Forest: Developers, Destroyers and Defenders of the Amazon* (London: Verso, 1989), pp. 37-40.

Profit From Rain Forest Products

Deals between banks and rain forest governments, many people believe, will never entirely stop rain forest destruction. The people of rain forest nations themselves must agree that careful management of rain forests will be, in the long run, better than cutting down the forests for development.

In many rain forest countries, plans are under-way to educate people about why they should care about preserving rain forests. They are learning, for example, that if too much land is cleared, heavy rains can cause mud slides that wipe out towns and villages and wash dirt into rivers and streams, killing fish. They are also learning that the forests shade the land from the hot tropical sun. If too much forest is cut down, the land can turn into useless desert. But just learning these things about the importance of rain forests is not enough. People also have to agree that the forests themselves have real, practical value.

One important way that forests are valuable is that they contain products people around the world want to buy. In recent years, the government of Brazil has set aside certain lands as *extractive reserves*. On these reserves, people are allowed to *extract*, or take out, things that grow naturally in the rain forest. Rubber is one product that is taken from these reserves. Rubber tappers and other forest settlers also gather fruits and nuts. Brazil nuts, which grow in the Amazon rain forests, are sold throughout the world.

Companies in other countries help support rain forest preservation when they use these products. Ben and Jerry's ice cream company, for example, placed large orders for Brazil nuts and cashews from the rain forest for its popular Rainforest Crunch ice cream. The company gave part of its profits on the ice cream back to rain forest preservation. The Body Shop, which sells cosmetics and lotions, uses rain forest plants in many of its products. These projects support *sustainable* use of the forest. A *sustainable use* is one that allows people to use parts of the forest for profit but does not destroy the forest.

Attracting Tourists

Some countries, such as Costa Rica, have found that tourism in rain forests can make the forests worth preserving. The rain forests in the mountains of Costa Rica, called cloud forests, attract many visitors each year to see beautiful birds and a stunning variety of butterflies.

In another Central American nation, Belize, farmers have found that howler monkeys can help them earn some extra income. The monkeys are a great attraction for tourists, mainly because of their lionlike roar. Howler monkeys live high in the canopy of the rain forest, swinging from tree to tree, searching for the fruit they like to eat. To survive, the monkeys need long stretches of unbroken forest. So the farmers of Belize, when they clear land for farms, are careful to leave an undisturbed "skyway" of trees that provide food for the monkeys. News of the project has drawn tourists to the area, and local people have found new jobs as guides and operators of bed-and-breakfast inns.[5]

In Rwanda, a nation in Africa, endangered mountain gorillas live in the rain forest. Because they are a great tourist attraction, people in Rwanda have set aside their habitat and tried to protect the gorillas from poachers, who kill the animals and sell their remains. Unfortunately, in the 1990s, civil war in Rwanda kept many tourists away.

Creating Biosphere Reserves

When rain forest nations set aside land for preservation, they cannot always post a "Keep Out" sign, especially when there are people living in poverty nearby. So many rain forest countries now have *biosphere* reserves that have zones for different kinds of activities. One of these zones, usually at the center of the reserve, is left untouched. The other zones form rings around this core. In the second ring is a *buffer zone*, in which tribespeople can gather plants for medicine or food, scientists can gather plants and animals for study, and tourists can take photographs. The next ring is a zone in which people can farm small plots and collect wood. Finally, in the outermost zone, people build houses and roads.[6] One important feature of these reserves is that the people who live there help preserve it.

The Kuna Wildlands Project in Panama is an example of tribal people taking the lead in forest preservation. The Kuna Indians, a group of about thirty thousand people, faced pressure from loggers and settlers who wanted to burn down the forest. The Kunas decided to take on managing and protecting their land, which covers about sixty small islands off the coast of Panama. They built guard stations and set up patrols around their reserve. They use the reserve to gather food, construction materials for their homes, products to sell, and medicinal plants. They set up a small tourist center with a restaurant and dormitory and a building that

*T*ourists ride through the middle layer of the rain forest canopy aboard the "Rain Forest Aerial Tram" in Costa Rica. Tourism is currently the nation's top industry.

acts as a base for scientists who come to study the rain forest. The Kuna raised funds from environmental organizations, and they learned how to use the law to help them protect their reserve.[7]

Big Business in Medicine

Another sustainable use of rain forests is mining them for medicines. This activity can provide millions of dollars in profits for pharmaceutical companies and rain forest nations. Rain forest plants and animals are already used in many medicines. A drug to reduce blood pressure, for example, comes from the same poisonous plant that tribal hunters in South America use to coat the tips of their arrows.

Many other important medicines come from rain forests, such as the nicotine in antismoking patches, anesthetics used in surgery, the digitalin used to treat heart problems, and drugs to treat everything from depression to diarrhea.[8] Many scientists are studying medicines used by tribal doctors, called *shamans*, who use plants, insects, and animals of the forest to treat all sorts of diseases.

Scientists and drug companies believe that many other cures, including medicines to fight cancer, AIDS, and even "new" diseases that could break out, may be waiting to be discovered in the rain forests. Many have made deals with rain forest countries that will preserve parts of the rain forest for study.

One danger in rich nations and big companies being involved in rain forest preservation is that sometimes they can take all the profits for themselves. They help themselves make money, but they do not help the people of rain forest nations. But partnerships between big companies and rain forest nations often can provide profits for both parties. Some of the best rain forest projects are ones that are created and run by the people of the rain forest nations alone.

Finding New Sources of Food and Income

One problem that has to be solved if rain forests are to be saved is how to feed the millions of people who live in rain forest countries. A group called New Forests Project teaches people how to raise more food for their families without using slash-and-burn farming. Instead, the farmers plant their crops in "alleys" between rows of rain forest. This method allows the land to be farmed for a much longer time than is possible with cleared land. Farmers report that an acre of land farmed in this way produces eight times the amount of crops.

In Costa Rica, where beef cattle ranches had already destroyed many acres of rain forest land, a plan to switch to dairy farming has saved more trees from being cut down. An environmental organization set up an experiment to raise dairy cattle in an area called Cariari. A paved road was built from Cariari to San Jose, the capital of Costa Rica, so farmers could get their milk to market quickly. The farmers also grow corn and bananas on their land. In shallow, plastic-lined pits, they mix corn stalks and banana leaves with cow manure to form compost. The compost is then used to fertilize the land so that grass and crops will grow. Whereas beef cattle need large grazing areas, dairy cattle graze on the same land year after year. Farmers make a steady income to feed their families, and the surrounding rain forest remains standing.[9]

A project in Panama involves another kind of animal. The green iguana, a good source of protein, has been hunted by forest people for centuries. But iguanas, like many other animals, were becoming scarce as forests were destroyed. So some people, such as scientist Dagmar Werner, became "iguana ranchers." Called "Iguana Mama" because of her successful project, Werner has built concrete tunnels where iguanas lay their eggs. She collects the eggs, hatches them in incubators, then releases them into her fenced "ranch."[10] Since Werner began her project in 1990, many other people have begun raising iguanas for their meat. Most release the young iguanas into the forest, where feeding

What Comes From Rain Forests?

Fibers. Bamboo and rattan for furniture; ramie for fabric and fishing lines; kapok for insulation and life jackets; raffia and jute for rope and basket-making

Food. Avocados, bananas, coconuts, mangoes, Brazil nuts, cashews, macadamia nuts, peppers, cola for soft drinks

Houseplants. Swiss cheese plant, Zebra plant, philodendron, rubber tree plant, and many more

Medicines. Curare to relax muscles before surgery; quinine to treat malaria; reserpine to treat high blood pressure; digitalin and digitoxin for heart problems; kaolin for anti-diarrhea medicines; nicotine for anti-smoking patches

Oils. Coconut oil for suntan lotion and candles; bay oil for perfume; camphor oil for perfume, soap, and disinfectant; palm oil for shampoo; tolu balsam oil for cosmetics and cough drops

Spices. Chili, cinnamon, cloves, ginger, nutmeg, paprika, sesame seeds, vanilla, black pepper

Wood. Teak, mahogany, and rosewood for plywood, furniture, packing cases, boat-building, salad bowls, and paneling; ebony for piano keys. Note: Many of the trees cut down for these purposes are endangered species. And often, large areas of forest are cut down to find very few trees that are useful to make these products

Lots of other things! Chicle latex for chewing gum (a popular gum brand is "Chiclets"); copal for paints and varnishes; gutta percha for golf ball covers; rubber latex for airplane tires

Source: Kenton Miller and Laura Tangley, *Trees of Life: Saving Tropical Forests and Their Biological Wealth* (Boston: Beacon Press, 1991).

stations are set up to keep the lizards nearby. Scientists estimate that the meat from iguanas provides far more protein per acre, at far less cost, than beef cattle provide. And iguana ranching does not destroy rain forests![11]

Cutting Down Only Some Trees?

In some parts of the world, such as Indonesia, *selective* logging seems like an obvious way to save rain forests. In this process, loggers cut down only certain trees, the ones that will bring high prices on world markets. But, scientists say, selective logging often does not work. For one thing, loggers have to go deeper and deeper into the forest to find the trees they want to cut. To do that, they have to build roads, which results in forest destruction. And unless the forests are managed carefully to ensure that trees are replanted, the delicate balance of life in the forest can be permanently damaged.[12]

Finding Out More About Rain Forests

Years ago, scientists assumed all the soil in rain forests was rich and fertile. Now they know that is not true. But they are discovering that in some areas, the soil beneath rain forests might provide good land for farms and even fairly large tree plantations. If scientists can identify these areas, they could provide people with a good way to raise food and agricultural products to sell for many years—without cutting down additional rain forest.

Scientists are also trying to find out just how much rain forest needs to be saved so that a particular kind of environment will survive. The governments of some rain forest countries have set aside areas for experiments. Rain forests are broken up into "islands" of various sizes. Then the scientists study what happens to the wildlife living in each island over time. Already, scientists have discovered that the smallest islands do not survive—at least not with the same plant and animal species that once lived there. That is because the forest is exposed on all sides to the wind and sun. Low-growing plants and the insects and birds that feed on them begin to take over. The forest floor, which would normally be dark and almost free of plants, becomes tangled with undergrowth that saps nourishment from large trees.[13] And small forest islands are just that— islands. They are cut off from other parts of the forest, so plant and animal species from the larger forest cannot find their way there to help sustain the balance of life.

Do Rain Forests Have a Future?

Many of the efforts to save and manage rain forests are just beginning. Projects like biosphere reserves, iguana ranches, and farming on small plots of land are hopeful signs. But all too often, the drone of chain saws still drowns out the bird calls and the smoke from burning forests darkens the sky.

Chapter 6

Using or Conserving Rain Forests?

The debate continues over the world's rain forests. Are they more valuable being conserved to promote greater biodiversity and a better global environment? Or are they of greater benefit being cleared for lumber production and farming? Both sides of the conflict have justification for their views on this important issue.

Conserving Rain Forests

Sometimes, when rain forest destruction is not making headlines, it is easy to forget that tropical rain forests even exist. Recently, however, people were reminded of the damage that can be caused after rain forests are cleared. In late 1998, when Hurricane Mitch roared across the Caribbean Sea and struck Central America, thousands of people were killed in mud slides. According to researcher Seth Dunn of the Worldwatch Institute, this widespread destruction would not have happened if the land had still been covered by the rain forest. Dunn explains that the forests act like a sponge to absorb heavy rain slowly. When forests are destroyed, he says, it is a like turning up the "faucets" and throwing away the "sponges." The water can do nothing but rush full force across the land, wiping out roads, farms, factories, and people.[1]

Today, the rapid growth of the world population and the increasing demands for natural resources threaten many tropical rain forests. People have destroyed large areas of rain forests by clearing land for farms and cities. Massive mining, ranching, and timber projects also have caused large amounts of damage. Scientists estimate that 50 million acres of tropical rain forests are destroyed yearly. They fear that continuing destruction of the forest will kill off hundreds of thousands of valuable plant and animal species.

Using Rain Forests

Native people have lived in the rain forests for thousands of years without destroying them. In poor, overcrowded countries, rain forests are a source of wealth. The governments of these countries hope the rain forests will provide homes for the homeless, food for the hungry, and resources to sell to other countries. For them, the economic benefits of the rain forests far outweigh any environmental damage that would be done.

Arguments on Both Sides

Some people say rain forest land should be preserved at all costs. Others say development of rain forest land is important for the people of rain forest nations. Here are some of the major arguments on each side.

What people who want to preserve the rain forests believe.

➤Millions of plants and animals in tropical rain forests haven't yet been discovered, and they could provide cures for many diseases.

➤The trees of the rain forests are valuable to everyone in the world because they absorb carbon dioxide. The fewer trees there are, the more carbon dioxide there is in the atmosphere, which could increase global warming.

➤Clearing and logging in tropical rain forests should be banned because once the trees are gone, they will never grow back.

➤International banks and foreign companies should stop lending money to rain forest countries for development projects like dams and mines that destroy large areas of forest.

➤When rain forests are cut down, tribal peoples who have lived in the forest for centuries are often driven off their land.

➤Rain forests help provide food, clean water, and clean air for the people who live in or near them.

What people who want to develop the rain forests believe.

➤The plants and animals of the rain forest are not as valuable as the people who live in rain forest countries. Their needs should be considered first.

➤Countries like the United States, which have many cars, contribute much more to global warming than the burning of the rain forests does.

➤Many people in rain forest countries live in poverty. Growing crops for even a few seasons and cutting trees to sell to other countries helps them survive.

➤Rain forest countries need help if they are to modernize. How can they do that if they cannot use their land for industry?

➤In many other parts of the world, including the United States, tribal people have been driven off their land as settlers moved in. Those people can learn new ways and become part of modern civilization.

➤As forests make way for development, people can find more efficient ways to produce food, use available water, and ensure that the air remains clean.

Introduction

1. Kenton Miller and Laura Tangley, *Trees of Life: Saving Tropical Forests and Their Biological Wealth* (Boston: Beacon Press, 1991), pp. 68–69.

Chapter 1.   What Is a Tropical Rain Forest?

1. "Biogeography" entry in *Compton's Encyclopedia* (online).

2. John Terbough, *Diversity and the Tropical Rain Forest* (New York: Scientific American Library, 1992), pp. 10, 15.

3. *The World Almanac and Book of Facts, 1993* (New York: World Almanac: An imprint of Pharos Books, 1992).

4. Mark W. Moffett, *The High Frontier: Exploring the Tropical Rainforest Canopy*, p. 12 (from foreword by E.O. Wilson).

5. *The International Book of the Forest* (New York: Mitchell Beazley Publishers: An imprint of Simon & Schuster, 1981), p. 82.

6. Terbough, p. 5.

7. Susanna Hecht and Alexander Cockburn, *The Fate of the Forest: Developers, Destroyers and Defenders of the Amazon* (London: Verso, 1989), p. 24.

8. Andrew Revkin, *The Burning Season* (Boston: Houghton Mifflin Company, 1990), p. 26.

9. Bob Reiss, *The Road to Extrema* (New York: Summit Books, 1992), p. 26.

10. *The International Book of the Forest*, p. 80.

11. Steven R. Kellert, ed., *Macmillan Encyclopedia of the Environment*, vol. 2 (New York: Simon & Schuster and Prentice-Hall International, 1997), p. 120.

12. John Nichol, *The Mighty Rain Forest* (London: David & Charles, 1990), pp. 29, 67.

13. *The International Book of the Forest*, p. 91.

14. *Zoo Guides: The Rainforest* (CD) (San Diego, Calif.: REMedia, Inc., 1994).

15. Adrian Forsyth and Kenneth Miyata, *Tropical Nature* (New York: Charles Scribner's Sons, 1984), pp. 54–56.

Chapter 2.   Who Owns the Forests?

1. John Terbough, *Diversity and the Tropical Rain Forest* (New York: Scientific American Library, 1992), p. 44.

2. Kenton Miller and Laura Tangley, *Trees of Life: Saving Tropical Forests and Their Biological Wealth* (Boston: Beacon Press, 1991), p. 85.

3. John Nichol, *The Mighty Rain Forest* (London: David & Charles, 1990), p. 151.

4. Miller and Tangley, p. 97.

5. William W. Bevis, *Borneo Log: The Struggle for Sarawak's Forests* (Seattle: University of Washington Press, 1995), p. 115.

6. Bob Reiss, *The Road to Extrema* (New York: Summit Books, 1992), p. 147.

7. Ibid., p. 30.

8. *Zoo Guides: The Rainforest* (CD) (San Diego, Calif.: REMedia, Inc., 1994).

9. Irving Mintzer and James Hansen, "The Greenhouse Effect Is Real," in Matthew Polesetsky, ed., *Global Resources: Opposing Viewpoint Series* (San Diego, Calif.: Greenhaven Press, 1991), p. 57.

10. Andrew C. Revkin, "The Greenhouse Effect Will Result in Disaster," in Polesetsky, ed., p. 75.

11. Ibid.

Chapter 3. "A Land Without People for a People Without Land"

1. John Nichol, *The Mighty Rain Forest* (London: David & Charles, 1990), p. 138.

2. Kenton Miller and Laura Tangley, *Trees of Life: Saving Tropical Forests and Their Biological Wealth* (Boston: Beacon Press, 1991), p. 53.

3. Bob Reiss, *The Road to Extrema* (New York: Summit Books, 1992), p. 32.

4. *The World Almanac and Book of Facts, 1993* (New York: World Almanac: An imprint of Pharos Books, 1992).

5. Susanna Hecht and Alexander Cockburn, *The Fate of the Forest: Developers, Destroyers and Defenders of the Amazon* (London: Verso, 1989), pp. 102–103.

6. Ibid., p. 108.

7. Andrew Revkin, *The Burning Season* (Boston: Houghton Mifflin Company, 1990), pp. 111–112.

8. Ibid., pp. 112–113.

9. Hecht and Cockburn, p. 110.

10. Ibid.

11. Reiss, pp. 144–145.

12. Hecht and Cockburn, pp. 110–112.

13. Revkin, pp. 115–117.

14. Hecht and Cockburn, p. 112.

15. Miller and Tangley, p. 66.

16. Ibid., pp. 67–68.

17. Revkin, pp. 114–115.

18. Miller and Tangley, p. 63.

Chapter 4. Battles Over Rain Forests

1. Marlise Simons, "Vast Amazon Fires, Man–Made, Linked to Global Warming," *The New York Times*, August 12, 1989, p. A1.

2. Frederic Golden, "A Catbird's Seat on Amazon Destruction," *Science*, October 13, 1989, p. 201.

3. Eugene Linden, "Playing with Fire," *Time*, September 18, 1989, p.76.

4. Simons, p. A6.

5. Susanna Hecht and Alexander Cockburn, *The Fate of the Forest: Developers, Destroyers and Defenders of the Amazon* (London: Verso, 1989), p. 37.

6. Linden, p. 76.

7. Michael S. Serrill, "A Dubious Plan for the Amazon," *Time*, April 17, 1989, p. 67.

8. William W. Bevis, *Borneo Log: The Struggle for Sarawak's Forests* (University of Washington Press: Seattle, 1995), pp. 140–142.

9. Wade Davis, Ian Mackenzie, and Shane Kennedy, *Nomads of the Dawn: The Penan of the Borneo Rainforest* (Pomegranate Artbooks, 1995).

10. Kenton Miller and Laura Tangley, *Trees of Life: Saving Tropical Forests and Their Biological Wealth* (Boston: Beacon Press, 1991), p. 73.

11. Ibid., p. 72.

12. Ibid., p. 97.

13. Bob Reiss, *The Road To Extrema* (New York: Summit Books, 1992), pp. 147–166.

Chapter 5. What Is It Worth to Save Rain Forests?

1. Bob Reiss, *The Road to Extrema* (New York: Summit Books, 1992), p. 147.

2. Ibid., p. 150.

3. Ibid., pp. 147–166.

4. Kenton Miller and Laura Tangley, *Trees of Life: Saving Tropical Forests and Their Biological Wealth* (Boston: Beacon Press, 1991), p. 62.

5. Judith Gradwohl and Russell Greenberg, *Saving the Tropical Forests* (London: Earthscan Publications, Limited, 1988), pp. 72–75.

6. James D. Nations, "Protected Areas in Tropical Rainforests," in Suzanne Head and Robert Heinzman, eds., *Lessons of the Rainforest*, (Sierra Club Books: San Francisco), 1990, pp. 214–215.

7. Gradwohl and Greenberg, pp. 81–83. Information also gathered from *Tropical Forests: A Call for Action*, Report of an International Task Force Convened by the World Resources Institute, the World Bank, and the U.N. Development Project, 1985, p. 39.

8. Reiss, pp. 80, 90.

9. Gradwohl and Greenberg, pp. 116–118.

10. "Iguana Mama," *International Wildlife*, September/October 1989, pp. 24–27.

11. Gradwohl and Greenberg, pp. 118–122.

12. Ibid., pp. 30–31.

13. Susanna Hecht and Alexander Cockburn, *The Fate of the Forest: Developers, Destroyers and Defenders of the Amazon* (London: Verso, 1989), pp. 37–40.

Chapter 6. Using or Conserving Rain Forests?

1. Donna Abu-Nasr, "Extreme Weather Bears Human Fingerprint," *The Star-Ledger*, November 28, 1998, p. 2.

Books

Kaplan, Elizabeth. *Temperate Forest*. New York: Benchmark Books: Marshall Cavendish, 1996.

Pulley Sayer, April. *Tropical Rain Forest*. New York: Twenty–First Century Books: A Division of Henry Holt & Company, 1994.

Tangley, Laura. *The Rainforest*. New York: Chelsea House Publishers, 1992.

Warburton, Lois. *Rainforests*. San Diego, Calif.: Lucent Books, Lucent Overview Series—Our Endangered Planet, 1991.

Internet Addresses

Conservation International. April 29, 1999. <http://www.conservation.org/> (May 3, 1999).

Gaia Forest Conservation Archives. n.d. <http://forests.org> (May 3, 1999).

Rain Forest Aerial Tram of Costa Rica. 1999. <http://www.rainforesttram.com/> (May 3, 1999).

Rainforest Action Network. n.d. <http://www.ran.org/ran/> (May 3, 1999).

Rainforest Concern. n.d. <http://rainforest.org.uk/> (May 3, 1999).

Index